At the Top

Written by Holly Woolnough

Illustrated by Stu McLellan

Collins

Bess and Ted sit at the top.

Dad hops on the bus.

4

The full bus sets off.

The reds run and kick.

Can it hit the back of the net?

The men huff and puff.

9

Mum pats the red dog in the sun.

11

At the dock, Dad gets a big cod.

15

🐾 Review: After reading 🐾

Use your assessment from hearing the children read to choose any GPCs, words or tricky words that need additional practice.

Read 1: Decoding

- Turn to page 6. Ask the children to point to and read the word that begins with the sound /r/. (*reds, run*)
- Ask the children to point to the digraphs for the phoneme /c/ in the words: **kick**, **back**.
- Challenge the children to read page 10. Say: Can you sound out the words in your head silently, before reading them aloud?
- Look at the "I spy sounds" pages (14–15). How many objects can the children point out that contain the /b/ sound? (e.g. *brown, bird, bus, ball, bank, boats, blocks/buildings, bridge, building site, builders*)

Read 2: Prosody

- Model reading the main text on page 12, pausing at the comma.
- Point out how the comma separates where the picture is (**At the dock**) and what Dad does.
- Ask individual children to read the sentence, checking they pause at the correct place.

Read 3: Comprehension

- Ask the children: Have you looked out of a high-up window? Is your bedroom high up? What do you see below?
- Turn to pages 4 and 5 and focus on the picture. Ask: Are we looking at the street from the bottom or top of a building? (*top*) How do you know? (*we can see the tops of things as if we're looking down at them*)
- On page 8, point to **huff and puff**. Ask: Why do the men huff and puff? (e.g. *they are working hard/ carrying heavy bricks*) Encourage the children to huff and puff as they act out carrying a heavy weight.
- Turn to pages 14–15 and check children's understanding of vocabulary by asking them to find the following: an orange bus; children in their kit; a window at the top; the dock.